TEXAS

A PICTURE BOOK TO REMEMBER HER BY

Designed by
DAVID GIBBON

Produced by
TED SMART

CRESCENT

INTRODUCTION

Until 1959, when Alaska joined the Union, Texas was the largest state of the U.S.A., its vast area of some 262,840 square miles separated from Mexico in the southwest by the fifth longest river of North America, the Rio Grande, which flows from the Rocky Mountains to the Gulf of Mexico. Most of its eastern boundary with Louisiana is formed by the Sabine River, while the Red River in the north makes up approximately two thirds of the boundary with Oklahoma.

According to archaeological evidence, the first inhabitants of Texas lived in camps 37,000 years ago, but it was not until 1528 that the first white man stepped onto Texan soil. He was a Spaniard, Alvar Núñez Cabeza de Vaca, who, with three companions, survived a shipwreck off the Gulf Coast. An account of his adventures is the first written record in Texan history.

The first real explorers of this part of the continent, however, arrived in 1540 and were followers of Hernando de Soto, led by Francisco Vásquez de Coronado, a Spanish soldier and, in spite of enormous difficulties, they travelled in search of the mythical "Seven Cities of Gold".

Since the 16th century Spanish influence on Texas has been profound, with the first Missions established in the east by about 1690 and, although by the end of the century most had been abandoned in face of Indian hostility, by 1730 more than thirty Spanish expeditions had ventured into the open land, founding three permanent settlements at San Antonio, Nacogdoches and Goliad, before the beginning of 1800. The Spaniards were also responsible for introducing not only their language into their New World Province, which included present day New Mexico, Arizona and California, but continued their traditional methods of ranching, introducing both horses and cattle to Texan soil.

The French too came to look for new land in Texas, as Louisiana and Illinois had already been annexed to the Crown of France through the achievement of the great Mississippi explorer, Robert Cavelier, sieur de La Salle. His final expedition led him to Matagorda Bay on the Texas coast, an inlet which he had supposed was the western outlet of the Mississippi River. Realizing his mistake he made an unsuccessful attempt, with his dwindling party, to reach Canada and on his subsequent endeavour his men mutinied and he was assassinated.

In 1821, after the Mexican Revolution, the former outpost of San Antonio became a part of Mexico and in the same year Stephen F. Austin, after whom the present capital of Texas is named, arrived there to arrange, through the government, for 300 families to be admitted into Texas from the U.S.A., on a grant of 200,000 acres. Other grants were soon approved and by 1832 the numbers of Anglo-American settlers had increased to such a considerable extent that three years later the Texans formed a provisional government and in 1836 issued a declaration of independence.

That very year, in a desperate bid to gain control of San Antonio and so establish their independence from Mexico, the town's most famous building was the scene of a siege that was to have a dramatic effect on the history of Texas – the Battle of the Alamo. The Alamo, originally the 18th century Franciscan Mission of San Antonio de Valero, had been abandoned like many similar missions and was for a time occupied by Spanish troops who had called it the Alamo – the Spanish name for the grove of cotton wood in which it stood. On the 23rd of February, 1836, about 187 brave men, including Jim Bowie, William B. Travis and the legendary Davy Crockett defended the Alamo against an army of 14,000 Mexicans, while Texan settlers formed themselves into a military force. For twelve days they bravely held out, but on March 6th the Mexicans breached the walls and killed all inside. The defenders, however, did not yield without an intense struggle and the Mexican losses were estimated at between 1,000 and 1,600 men.

Six weeks later the Texan military commander, Sam Houston, followed the Mexican army northwards and with a surprise attack on San Jacinto, defeated the army and captured their leader, the Dictator Santa Anna, securing victory for the Texans.

For a time the Alamo was used by the U.S. for quartering troops and storing supplies, but has now been restored and together with its adjacent buildings is maintained as an historic site and a memorial to the men who died there.

In 1845 Texas became a state of the Union, but its role in the Confederacy during the Civil War was not a particularly important one, and although Texas supplied men, material and services the state itself saw little action. However, it did suffer both economically and politically afterwards. Real recovery did not occur until the turn of the century when great strides were made in railroad building, shipping and manufacturing. A major breakthrough in 1901, when a huge oil gusher erupted at Spindletop, near the city of Beaumont, marked the start of the state's prosperity and Texas is now the leading U.S. oil producer, with approximately 40% of the nation's proved reserves. From the rich oil strikes developments have been made in petrochemical industries and, in addition the steel mills, electronics industries, (including those associated with many spaceflight centres), cattle ranching and the growing of cotton, rice and peanuts, have all contributed to the prosperous Texan economy.

The scenery of this thriving American state is as diverse as the crops that are grown there. In the east are forests of pine and cypress, whilst in the west are treeless plains, sagebrush, mesquite and the dense-turfed buffalo grass. To the south, along the Gulf of Mexico, stretch flat prairies and from San Antonio to the Mexican borders cattle ranches, whitewashed villages, palm trees and orange groves are a familiar sight in the Rio Grande Valley.

Amongst the cities Houston is now the largest and it is famous for its Manned Space Centre and Astrodomain, comprising Astrohall, Astroworld and Astrodome: Austin, the state capital and Waco are also important centres, whilst Dallas and Fort Worth, in close proximity to each other, contain all the skyscrapers and multi-laned freeways that are a feature of so many modern American cities.

In the Inner Space Cavern, Georgetown, light glistens on the subterranean beauty of stalactites and stalagmites.

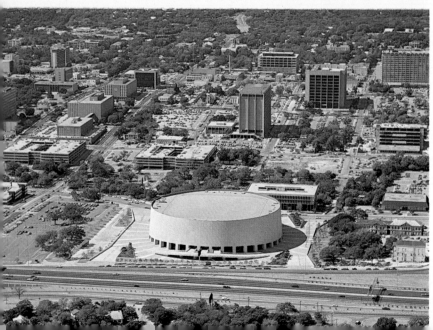

Once the riverside village of Waterloo, built where the River Colorado crosses the Balcones Escarpment, Austin today *on these pages* is the flourishing capital of Texas. With the harnessing of the river for flood control and power in the early 20th century Austin became a centre of research and development, at the very heart of which stands the magnificent pink granite State Capitol building *right,* a classical structure in the shape of a Greek cross, which was completed in 1888.

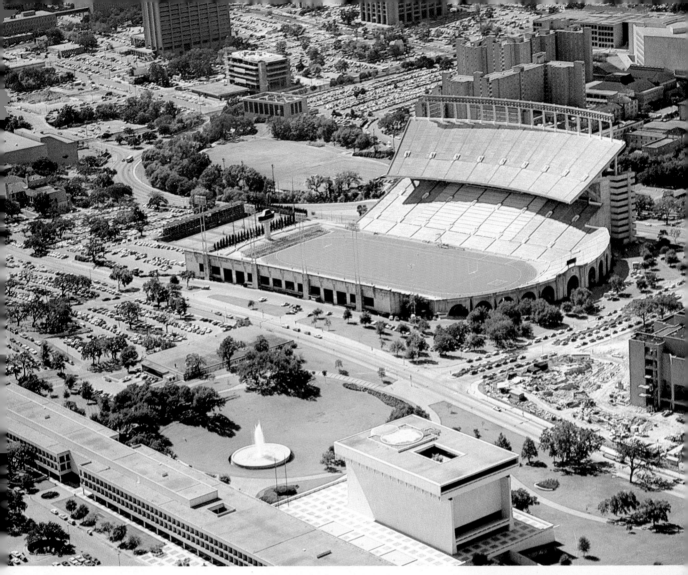

Presiding over the ornate dome of the State Capitol, the Goddess of Liberty *left* stands over 300 feet above the ground.

The University of Texas has contributed greatly to the cultural life of Austin. Its extensive campus includes, next to the stadium *above*, the L. B. Johnson Library in which the public papers of the 36th U.S. President are housed, the imposing tower of the administrative building *right* and the Littlefield Fountain *below*.

Overleaf: A view of the State Capitol from Congress Avenue.

THERE IS NO DANGER OF   THE TEXAS RANGERS
A SURPRISE   HAVE DONE
WHEN THE RANGERS ARE   ALL THAT COULD BE ASKED
BETWEEN US AND THE ENEMY   OR REQUIRED OF SOLDIERS

On the Capitol grounds stand a series of memorial statues. The Goddess of Liberty *above* marks the spot where the Bicentennial Capsule is buried. The bronze 'Hiker' *right* honours the memory of Spanish-American War Veterans and the figure of a soldier *below* commemorates the Alamo heroes. 'Mustangs' *below right* is a tribute to the significant role of these magnificent creatures. The five figures on the Confederate Memorial *below far right* represent the Infantry, Cavalry, Artillery, Navy and President Jefferson Davis. In recognition of Terry's Rangers, the statue *left* was sculpted by Pompeo Coppini.

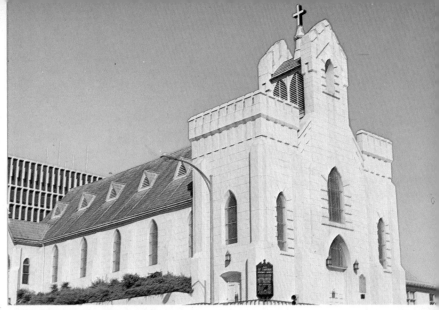

Austin is a city of contrasts, in which the old coexists with the new. Beside breathtaking products of modern expansion like the First Federal Plaza *left* stand stately mansions such as that shown *right* or the Texas Governor's mansion *below right*, which with its dignified columns and broad verandas recalls the era when the Republic of Texas was in the making. The Old Bakery *below* dates back to 1876 and St David's Episcopal Church *above right* is also firmly rooted in Texas history. Even the street signs *above and top* bear witness to the fact that in the interests of growth, the traditional has not been lost.

Dallas *on these pages,* the state's second largest city, is also the Southwest's largest banking centre, leader in wholesale business and among the leaders in 'million dollar' companies. Dallas is a transport and communications hub where soaring skyscrapers rise from a giant throbbing web of ultramodern highways.

Among the city's most popular sporting events are the football games of the Dallas Cowboys, perhaps best known for their Cotton Bowl Football Classic on New Year's Day.

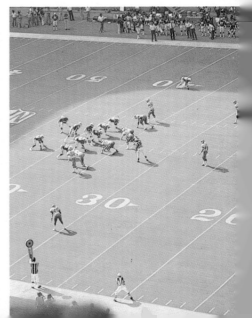

At night Dallas offers all the exhilaration and entertainment of a dynamic metropolis: *above left*, The Whiskey River Country and Western Club, *above right*, The Elan Nightclub and Disco, *left and far left*, Baby Doll's Matchless Mine and *right*, Pawn Shop Club and Disco.

The American Culinary Art Show in the Dallas
Convention Center creates a gourmet's paradise
with a mouthwatering display of masterpieces
designed to titillate the eye as much as the palate.

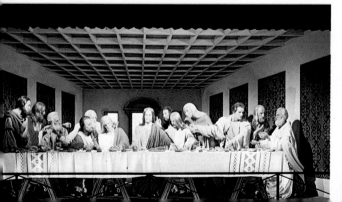

In the Grand Prairie, Texas, one hundred and eighty famous characters bring one of the world's most colourful histories to life at the Southwestern Historical Wax Museum. Here the most famous of past and present heroes, statesmen, film stars and rogues, sculptured in life-size wax, each with imported medical eyes and human hair inserted one strand at a time, are displayed in historically accurate settings.

The people of Dallas pursue culture and historical interest with as much enthusiasm as business. The Dallas Symphony Orchestra *above right,* founded in 1900 as a 40 member ensemble is now one of the United States' major orchestras. In the Olla Padrida *below right* a portrait artist works in the handmade crafts centre. *Left and above left* the stained glass windows of Trinity Methodist Church, now used as a theatre, provide authentic turn-of-the-century atmosphere for a production of Theatre Onstage *above.* One of the historical buildings in the Old City Park *below* provides a nostalgic glimpse of Dallas' past.

Dallas has preserved its past in its fine stately mansions *above left*, in the pioneer buildings of the Old City Park *below* and *centre left*, and in the retention of historical monuments: the log cabin in Elm Street *above* was once inhabited by Neely Bryan, founder of Dallas. The Clocktower *top* and the European Crossroads Café *right* create an Old World atmosphere which is recaptured *below left* in the unique artists' market of the Olla Podrida.

The magnificent views of Houston *on these pages and overleaf* convey something of the magnitude and the dynamism of Texas' largest city. The statue *below* commemorates the city's namesake, Sam Houston, leader of the struggle by U.S. emigrants in Mexican territory to make Texas part of the United States.

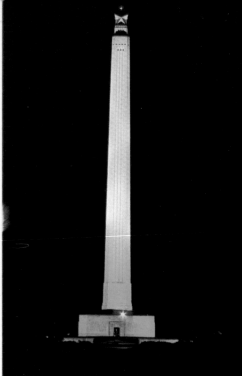

Among Houston's many attractions, old and new are: *above left*, the Summit Stadium, *above*, the San Jacinto Monument, *below*, one of many exhibits in the Contemporary Arts Museum, *bottom*, the Battleship Texas, only survivor of the dreadnought class, *below left*, the 36 million dollar 'Eighth wonder of the world', the Astrodome, *left*, the library of the University of Houston, *overleaf*, the interior of the giant Galleria complex. The sun sets *right* over the Houston skyline.

Houston by night becomes a vast recreation ground with a seemingly endless range of atmospheres and tempos: *left,* the plush interior of the Great Caruso Restaurant, *above,* a spectacular firework display in the Astroworld Amusement Park, *right,* the Boogie Fog Disco in Astroworld on Halloween night, *below right,* the Bowany Restaurant, *below,* the Anhauser Busch Brewery, *bottom,* the Ritz Nightclub Disco, *below left,* Hugo's Windowbox in the Hyatt Regency Hotel.

Crowds throng the Summit Stadium *on these pages* for the Houston Rockets versus New York basketball game.

On the banks of the Houston Ship Channel which connects the city with the Gulf of Mexico, industrial buildings *overleaf* stand silhouetted against the evening sky.

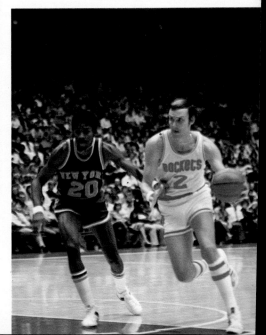

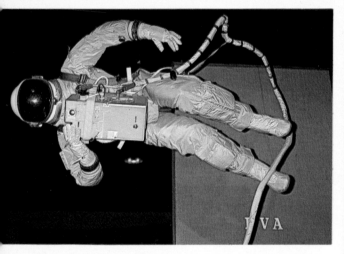

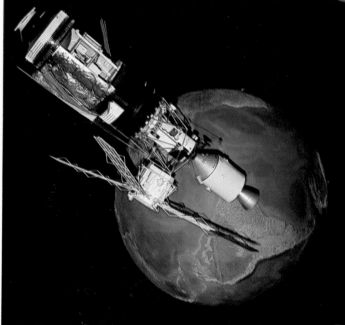

The Lyndon B. Johnson Space Center, one of the newest and largest research and development facilities of the National Aeronautics and Space Administration, is the focal point for the nation's manned space flight. Here spacecraft that have been to the moon and back are on display for all to see.

LUNAR MODULE TEST ARTICLE
LTA-8

UNITED
STATES

The Astrodome or Harris County Domed Stadium *left* is the world's first air-conditioned domed stadium for baseball matches and virtually any other sporting event. Part of the Astrodomain, the stadium seats up to 66,000 and could contain an 18 storey building. It is the home of baseball's National League Houston Astros, seen *below and right* playing the Giants.

The Rice Stadium *above* provides yet another magnificent setting for football games.

The Texas Cyclone roller coaster *above* forms part of the Houston Astroworld.

Houston's Zoological Gardens *above left* feature amongst other attractions a perfect reconstruction of the natural habitat of the gorilla.

The city's Museum of Natural Science *left* is one of the largest in the southwest.

An alligator *below left* emerges from the waters of the See-arama Marineworld, Galveston Island.

Houston, Botanical Gardens and Arboretum *below* provide a centre for the study of conservation and field botany.

Moonlight dapples the offshore waters of Corpus Christi *right*.

The Alabama-Coushatta Indian Reservation *above and left* provides colourful evidence of the state's historical heritage and love of history again finds its expression *below,* as two young Texans parade in costumes at the Renaissance Festival, Plantersville.

The Huntsville prison Rodeo *above left and below left* includes such spectacular events as bull-riding and saddle and bareback bronc riding.

Beyond the concrete congestion of the cities lie the beautiful rugged Hill Country, traditional haunt of the Longhorn *right,* and the Pernales State Park on the banks of the Pernales River *above right.*

THE ORIGINAL BUILDING
FIRST BAPTIST CHURCH
1889 - 1908

The original Baptist church *left* dates back to the days when Amarillo was a natural stopping place for the cattle trails which crossed the Panhandle of Texas. Today livestock still have a significant role to play and the sale of cattle *below right* is undertaken with a degree of ceremony. Amarillo has retained its 'Western' atmosphere: an intricately decorated saddle *above* awaits purchase in one of the saddle shops and a brightly coloured stage coach *below* advertises a steak ranch.

The railway station *above right* and St Joseph's Church *centre right* in San Angelo recall the days when the town grew up as a centre of early ranching efforts.

The thriving cosmopolitan centre of San Antonio *above* at night becomes a vast panorama of sparkling lights. Downtown San Antonio *left* is remarkable for its towering modern structures but much is owed to its Spanish Colonial and Mexican ancestry, reflected *above right* in the architecture of the Landmark Building.

The sunken gardens in Brackenridge Park *below right* are masterpieces of floral design.

At the city centre stands the Alamo *below, overleaf left and overleaf right,* an 18th-century Franciscan mission where the legendary Texan defenders, including Davy Crockett and Jim Bowie, were purportedly massacred.

Texas is a state of awe-inspiring natural beauty. Amidst the Davis Mountains, the Sawtooth *above* rises 7748 ft. Pulliam Ridge *right* forms a spectacular edge of the Chisos Basin and Hunter Peak *below* ranks among the highest Guadalupe Mountains. The Palo Duro Canyon *left* presents a rugged panorama of changing colours and patterns.

Overleaf: Sunset transforms a Gasoline Plant near Kermit.

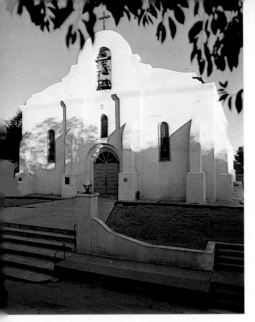

In the far west corner of Texas, below a narrow pass, where the Rio Grande issues from the bare southernmost spurs of the Rockies, lies El Paso with its dramatic blending of American and Mexican cultures, *below and above right*. Masterpieces of modern architecture like the Civic Centre *right and below right* reach into the clear air while centuries-old mission bells still call the faithful. The mission of San Elizario *above* was founded in 1777 and is still active today.

The ever-changing colours of the evening sky *left* find sympathetic reflection in the waters of the Red River as it wends its way through the Palo Duro Canyon.

The Rio Grande *overleaf* spills out into the international waters of the Amistad Lake.

First published in Great Britain 1979 by Colour Library International Ltd.
© Illustrations: Colour Library International Ltd, 163 East 64th Street, New York 10021.
Colour separations by La Cromolito, Milan, Italy.
Display and text filmsetting by Focus Photoset, London, England.
Printed by Cayfosa and bound by Eurobinder - Barcelona (Spain)
Published by Crescent Books, a division of Crown Publishers Inc.
Library of Congress Catalogue Card No. 78-74854
CRESCENT 1979